IMAGES
of America

NEW YORK STATE NATIONAL GUARD

On the cover: Members of the 5th Company and Howitzer Section of the famous 7th Regiment, National Guard, State of New York, pose in their gray fatigue blouses, trimmed with black, around 1885–1897. Note the regimental number painted on their knapsacks and a white, cork summer helmet, with regimental crest, visible inside the tent. This photograph's label reads, "Pach Bro's 841 B'WAY, N.Y." (Anthony Gero collection.)

IMAGES
of America

NEW YORK STATE NATIONAL GUARD

Anthony Gero and Roger Sturcke

ARCADIA
PUBLISHING

ISBN 978-0-7385-4936-1

Published by Arcadia Publishing
Charleston, South Carolina

Printed in the United States of America

Library of Congress Catalog Card Number: 2006931603

For all general information contact Arcadia Publishing at:
Telephone 843-853-2070
Fax 843-853-0044
E-mail sales@arcadiapublishing.com
For customer service and orders:
Toll-Free 1-888-313-2665

Visit us on the Internet at www.arcadiapublishing.com

We dedicate this work to those defenders of the Empire State and their families who served and still do. Lest we forget.

Contents

ACKNOWLEDGMENTS

No work of history can ever be accurately presented without the vital assistance of others, so we, as authors, collectors, and historians, wish to acknowledge the following who have, over the past 40 years, assisted us in the vineyards of military history: Col. John R. Elting (United States Army), Barry Thompson, Raymond Johnson, Eric Manders, Philip Maples, René Chartrand, Brian Dunnigan, Capt. Fitzhugh McMasters (United States Navy), Alan Archambault, Al Haarmann, Maj. Rick Ugino (New York National Guard), Gen. Robert Mulligan Sr. (New York National Guard), Joe Thatcher, Col. Ed Milligan (United States Army), Bob Gibson, Robert Mulligan Jr., William Gladstone, Michael McAfee, Col. Fred Todd (New York National Guard), Orton Begner, Dave Sullivan, Dale Bevier, Bill Jacobs, Joe LoPiccolo, and Charles Eddy. Additionally, Cayuga County historian Sheila Tucker, Cayuga Museum director Eileen McHugh, the Company of Military Historians, and Pam O'Neil at Arcadia Publishing were all of great assistance to us.

Finally to our wives, Linda and Joy, who, over the many years of our researching and collecting military history, have understood our passion to write about it, we humbly say thank you.

INTRODUCTION

From 1803 to 1861, the New York State Militia was one of the largest in the United States and consisted of two classes of units, the Volunteer Militia and the Enrolled Militia. The Volunteer Militia had companies labeled as grenadiers, light infantry, rifles, horse artillery, artillery, and cavalry who could afford the expenses to uniform themselves and train more regularly. Their ranks usually consisted of skilled workers, merchants, and landed gentry.

The Enrolled Militia was made up of all other able-bodied males of legal age who could carry a musket and do field duty. In theory, the Enrolled Militia stemmed from the Greek idea of a citizen army, modified in practice by British traditions of the 17th and 18th centuries and politicized by the American republican spirit. Usually the Enrolled Militia in New York State did not include African Americans, although during the War of 1812, the state did experiment with some units of African American men.

Resistance to the general levy on New York State's male population grew in the 1840s, and by the end of the decade, the Enrolled Militia was abolished and replaced with an expanded volunteer system. For example, the American Rifles, a four-battalion organization formed in New York City in the 1850s, evolved into the 71st Regiment (American Guard), New York State Militia, by 1860. In Troy, the Troy Citizen Corps, formed prior to the War of 1812, was an independent company until disbanded in 1864, as a result of many of its members volunteering for federal service; it was not until 1876 that the unit was able to re-create itself as the 6th Separate Company.

New York was the country's most populated state in 1861 and boasted the largest and best-organized militia. In 1861, the New York State Militia consisted of 8 divisions, 25 brigades, and 58 regiments. With the outbreak of the Civil War, the New York State Militia immediately sent 11 regiments to Washington, D.C., for three months of duty, while 7 other regiments volunteered for "three years or the war." These regiments became New York Volunteers regiments.

On April 23, 1862, New York State changed its militia's name from New York State Militia to National Guard, State of New York. For example, the famous 69th Regiment, New York State Militia, from New York City was now labeled as the 69th Regiment, National Guard, State of New York. Modern writers can find these name changes confusing; for instance, the 71st Regiment, New York State Militia, frequently photographed from 1860 to 1863, became the 71st Regiment, National Guard, State of New York, and should not be confused with the 71st New York Volunteers raised in 1861, also known as the 2nd Regiment, Excelsior Brigade (Jackson Light Infantry). The 71st New York Volunteers mustered out in 1864 but not the 71st Regiment, National Guard, State of New York, which remained in existence into the 20th century.

In 1862, 1863, and 1864, many National Guard, State of New York, regiments were called up for active service, ranging from one to three months. In the winter of 1862, two regiments served for nine months. During the war, the state kept enlarging its National Guard, State of New York, forces so that by 1866 it consisted of 8 divisions, 26 brigades, 95 regiments, and 8 batteries of artillery and squadrons of cavalry. For example, the 24th Brigade of National Guard, State of New York, was headquartered in Syracuse and covered the area from Syracuse to Watertown. The old 48th Regiment (Oswego County) and 51st Regiment (Onondaga County) were recruited up to authorized strength. Three new regiments were authorized for the brigade, the 75th, the 85th, and the 88th Infantry, plus a battery of artillery and a battalion of cavalry.

In 1863, a new-style state uniform was adopted with a choice of two patterns, a baggy "chasseur" uniform and a more-conservative cut "polka" uniform. These were piped in branch colors: white for infantry, red for artillery, orange for cavalry, and green for rifles. A distinctive cap piped with the unit's branch colors—with a New York State shield plate, unit number, and pom-pom of red, white, and blue—were called for. Often collectors and historians mistake these National Guard, State of New York, uniforms of 1863 for the M1861 New York State jackets worn by the New York Volunteers, which are similar in appearance.

When on active duty in 1861, mostly militia-style uniforms were worn. In the following years, United States Army uniforms were issued when members were called up for active duty, although some would continue to use their pre-1862 National Guard, State of New York, or 1863 state-issued uniforms. Finally, especially in the New York City and Albany regions, several commands had regimental uniforms that differed from these proscribed 1863 state-issued uniforms. As a result, those wishing to verify New York Militia, National Guard, State of New York, and New York Volunteer dress from 1860 to 1866 can find these years most vexing.

After 1865, many returning veterans wished to rejoin their old National Guard, State of New York, units. Many Irish Americans living in New York State, and Irish American veterans of the war, were sympathetic to the Fenian movement's Irish Republican Army. Along New York State's Canadian border, raids were staged in 1866 and 1870 by uniformed and un-uniformed Irish Republican Army members, while British, Canadian, and United States authorities struggled to stop open warfare. Often units of New York's military forces were called out to help maintain order along the border.

By 1865, the National Guard, State of New York, numbered about 50,000 men. In 1868, the New York legislature ordered it to be reduced to 30,000 men, and 49 regiments and 1 battery of artillery were disbanded. Further reductions took place over the next few years, especially in 1881, when the guard was reduced to between 15,000 and 20,000 men.

As the workers in New York State struggled for their rights in the 1870s, 1880s, and 1890s, numerous strikes and work stoppages occurred, especially on the railroads. Many times, it was the National Guard, State of New York, that was called to keep order. By the 1870s, New York's armed force was a vibrant organization, with many units wearing distinctive uniforms in a variety of colors and styles. Regiments of infantry, troops of cavalry, and batteries of artillery existed in almost all major cities and vital regions of the state. From Buffalo to Rochester, Auburn to Oswego, Syracuse to Watertown, and Albany to New York City, National Guard, State of New York, units were maintained.

The National Guard, State of New York, sustained 20 separate companies of infantry in smaller areas, such as Batavia, Lockport, Rome, Warsaw, Oneonta, Malone, and Utica. These separate companies evolved, dissolved, and then reappeared. For instance, the 6th Separate Company from Troy kept its numerical designation from 1877 to 1900, but the 29th and 38th Separate Companies from Oswego, formed in 1881, were consolidated in 1892 to form the 48th Separate Company.

After 1881, the 3rd Regiment of Cavalry from New York City was gone, as was the 5th Regiment of Infantry, which wore a distinctly Prussian-style uniform. In Albany, the 10th Regiment, whose lineage went back to the Civil War, was reduced to a battalion, and in the vital cities of Oswego, Auburn, Syracuse, and Rochester, their regiments of infantry, the 48th, 49th, 51st, and 54th, respectively, were reduced to one or two separate companies of infantry.

A notable exception to these cutbacks was the Buffalo area, where the 65th and 74th Regiments of Infantry were retained. One can assume that this was done due to the area's proximity to the Canadian border. Both of these regiments were active into the 20th century; the 74th Regiment became the 174th Regiment, New York, National Guard, in 1921. The 65th Regiment became the 106th Field Artillery in 1917 and evolved into the 106th Armored Field Artillery by February 1955.

During the Spanish-American War, the renamed National Guard, New York, responded. Entire regiments volunteered for federal service. The 71st Regiment, National Guard, New York, enlisted and became the 71st New York Volunteers. Selected separate companies were formed into volunteer regiments too, numbered 1 through 3. For example, the 2nd Separate Company (Auburn) became Company M, 2nd Battalion, 3rd Regiment, New York Volunteers. The 1st Regiment, New York Volunteers, probably had the most exotic adventure, being sent to the Hawaiian Islands for garrison duty.

By 1903, the federal government passed the Dick Act, which brought the nation's various National Guards up to United States Army standards. When Pres. Woodrow Wilson ordered United States forces to Texas and then into Mexico, one of the largest contingents of National Guard troops sent was from New York State. Serving along the Texas border and formed into the 6th Division, United States Army, New York State's guardsmen obtained some valuable service.

From 1870 to 1915, the official policy of New York State did not allow the service of African American New Yorkers. Even though some other states like Massachusetts, Connecticut, Rhode Island, Ohio, Illinois, Virginia, Georgia, and Alabama had allowed segregated units in their respective state forces, New York did not. Legislation was eventually passed to rectify this omission, only after considerable efforts of African American New Yorkers through the NAACP. In 1915, with the influence of key white New Yorkers, the segregated 15th Regiment of Infantry was formed.

When the United States entered World War I, the National Guard, New York, was federalized, and many of its regiments were called up, their designations changed to fit federal specifications. For example, the 7th Regiment was designated the 107th Infantry, United States Army, the 3rd Regiment became the 108th Infantry, United States Army, and the 15th Regiment became the 369th Infantry, United States Army.

The 6th Division was renumbered as the 27th Division, United States Army, and was still made up of National Guardsmen from New York. This division was eventually sent to France, where it fought bravely. The 369th Infantry, United States Army, was allocated to the army's segregated 93rd Division, whose units were split up and assigned to the French army. While serving with the French, the regiment achieved an outstanding combat record and earned several nicknames, including "the Hell Fighters."

The 42nd Division, American Expeditionary Force, known as the Rainbow Division, was a one-of-a-kind unit since it was made up of various state National Guard units. New York State's contribution was the famous 69th National Guard, New York, which became the 165th Infantry, United States Army, 42nd Division, American Expeditionary Force.

At home, the state formed the New York Guard to replace the federalized units. For example, the 3rd Regiment, New York Guard, was raised in Upstate New York, and the segregated 15th Regiment, New York Guard, was raised in New York City. Even New York's high school students were formed into cadet corps across the state. In Cayuga County, for instance, the 2nd Battalion, 11th Regiment, Infantry Corps of Cadets, was raised at Auburn High School.

Following World War I, those former National Guardsmen who wished to rejoin were accommodated as the New York, National Guard, was re-formed, restructured, and renamed. Even the segregated 369th Regiment was kept. For two decades, guardsmen trained and served, performing functions such as duty during a prison riot in December 1929 in Auburn and helping during the floods in the Elmira region in the 1930s.

With the elections in Germany in 1932, the threat of fascism spread. After the United States presidential election of 1940, federal legislation and money began to impact the status and training of various state National Guards. In 1940, many units and divisions of state National

Guards were called up for a major training in Alabama. The 27th Division, still assigned to New York State, was called to Fort McClellan, Alabama.

When the infamous events of December 7, 1941, burst the bubble of America's isolationism, the men of the New York, National Guard, were among the first to be called up. The 27th Division was sent to the Pacific and served there. Other New York, National Guard, units served in the 40th and 44th Infantry Divisions, United States Army. The men of the segregated 369th Regiment, which had become an antiaircraft regiment prior to 1940, were shuttled from post to post in New York, Massachusetts, and California, ostensibly for training. Eventually the 369th Regiment was sent to Hawaii, where it was reorganized and its men were scattered by transfer to other units. Thus, during World War II, the 369th Regiment, New York, National Guard, was not allowed to achieve a combat record that its parent unit had achieved in World War I.

Back in New York State, as early as 1940, the New York Guard was re-formed to replace the departing New York, National Guard, units. Serving again as a home-defense force, the volunteer movement to join the New York Guard gained momentum, and thousands joined its formations; New York Guard units formed across the state. In Buffalo, the 74th Regiment was created; in Rochester, the 21st Regiment was organized; in central New York State, the 3rd Regiment was set up; and by 1943, an African American regiment, the 15th Regiment, was formed in New York City.

The New York Guard was kept in place until 1949, when it was officially disbanded (then reestablished in the 1950s due to the Korean War). The New York, National Guard, was reorganized after the war, as units were reestablished as the cold war grew. The New York Air National Guard, which can trace its heritage to the 1st Aero Company, New York National Guard, of 1916, was expanded. Additional units were set up in central and western New York cities, such as Niagara Falls and Syracuse. Eventually the New York Air National Guard came under the command of the United States Air Force, which separated from the army in 1947.

The New York, National Guard, and New York Air National Guard saw many of their members serve during the Korean War. Many famous regiments still maintained their existence, such as the 107th Infantry (the old 7th Regiment), which was still very active. In that decade, the regiment even brought back its famous full-dress, gray and black uniforms for special events. Once again, the 7th Regiment's historic dress could be seen on the streets of New York City. In 2006, the regiment celebrated its 200th anniversary and still wears its full-dress gray uniforms on occasion.

With the beginning of the 1960s, our photographic history ends. We have done this for a couple of reasons. First, the French have a word, *élan*, and for us, that spirit is seen in the images between 1860 and 1960, and the character of those pictured fires the imagination. Second, the 1960s marks the period of the cold war, which, although historically important, holds little fascination for us.

We are under no illusions about war. As the Duke of Wellington reportedly said, "There is no such thing as a little war." Therefore, our desire is to present a portal from which the former defenders of New York State can be viewed and remembered.

—Anthony Gero and Roger Sturcke

One

The Civil War Era
1860–1869

In this pre–Civil War photograph, reproduced as a cabinet image in the 1880s, a soldier in the 20th Regiment, New York State Militia, wears his full-dress uniform in the 1850s. Because the original image was reversed, the *NY* on his belt plate and the 20 on his shako plate appear backward. This regiment was nicknamed the "Ulster Guard." The photographer's label reads, "Short's Studio, 161 Strand, Rondout." (Roger Sturcke collection.)

Taken in Auburn in front of the Western Exchange Hotel on June 3, 1859, this rare image shows Company A (Old Guard), 49th Regiment, New York State Militia. Continental-style blue and buff uniforms were adopted by some units in New York's military forces between 1851 and 1878. Many Company A members served during the Civil War in the volunteer regiments raised in Cayuga County. The city of Auburn was home and residence to Secretary of State William H. Seward and Underground Railroad conductor Harriet Tubman. (Charles Eddy collection.)

A private of the 6th Company, 7th Regiment (National Guard), New York State Militia, is seen in this carte de visite, which has a photographer's label of "C. D. Fredricks & Co." of New York City, around 1861–1864. The image shows the changes made to the 7th Regiment's gray-trimmed black fatigue uniform after its return from active duty at Washington, D.C. On the cap, the company number was replaced with the regimental number, and white belts were replaced with a single black belt. (Anthony Gero collection.)

This tintype shows three unidentified sergeants of either the 47th Regiment, New York State Militia, or the 47th New York Volunteers around 1861. They wear a mixture of blue and gray clothing with the number 47 visible but reversed due to processing of the original image. The 47th was a Brooklyn-based unit for the New York State Militia and the New York Volunteers. (Anthony Gero collection.)

This c. 1860–1861 daguerreotype was taken in Gowanda, which is near Buffalo. The subject is identified as George W. Bailey. He wears a gray fatigue uniform with black collar and cuff piping, which was the style of the 74th Regiment, New York State Militia (Buffalo), undress uniform. The 21st New York Volunteers (1st Buffalo Regiment) was issued the 74th Regiment's fatigue uniforms early in 1861, and it may be that uniform depicted here. (Anthony Gero collection.)

This carte de visite shows a New York soldier, probably of the New York State Militia, around 1860–1863. He wears a white belt and shoulder strap, usually associated with pre- or early-war New York State Militia styles. His *SNY* belt plate, a New York State Militia issue, is also visible. The backmark reads, "Bogardus, 363 Broadway, New York." (Anthony Gero collection.)

Labeled as taken by "S. C. Abbot, Hamilton, N.Y." around 1860–1863, another carte de visite shows a New York soldier who is probably also a member of the New York State Militia. He wears a white shoulder strap and belt with an *SNY* belt plate. Note the similarity in his dress to the previous soldier's uniform. (Anthony Gero collection.)

This carte de visite, which has a photographer's mark of "Moulton and Dopp, Rome," shows a drummer of New York's military forces wearing a dark blue "polka" jacket with white piping, one of several uniform styles that were adopted in 1863. His National Guard, State of New York, status is seen in his distinctive dark blue cap, which is piped with white and displays a metal New York shield plate. The cap's pom-pom is red, white, and blue. The drum appears to have a painted New York State shield device, but the glare's reflection does not reveal the drum's detailing. The 101st Regiment National Guard, State of New York, was from Rome. (Anthony Gero collection.)

Noted as having been taken by "W. G. Smith, Cooperstown, NY, Opposite Keyes' and Carr's Hotel," this unidentified soldier is probably in the National Guard, State of New York, around 1863–1868. His distinctive kepi is the pattern adopted by the National Guard, State of New York, in 1863, as is his polka jacket. His regimental number is blurred in the original carte de visite photograph, but the 39th and 41st Regiments were based near Cooperstown. (Anthony Gero collection.)

The 10th Regiment, National Guard, State of New York, based in Albany, volunteered for active duty under Pres. Abraham Lincoln's call for nine-month volunteers in 1862. It entered United States service as the 177th New York Volunteer Infantry and served from November 1862 to September 1863. This image is identified as 1st Lt. Richard Strong, who died of typhoid on May 12, 1863. (Roger Sturcke collection.)

This second image reads, "Jonas R. Simmons 3 Corporal Co F 177 Regiment NYV." Notice the federal-issued clothing. Corporal Simmons wears a stripe on his trousers, which denotes his noncommissioned-officer status. There is no photographer's mark on this carte de visite image. (Roger Sturcke collection.)

The photographer's backmark on this carte de visite reads, "D. Deninson's Gallery, 57 State Street, Albany, NY." Notice the 10 and A on this soldier's forage cap. These pieces of photographic evidence indicate that the soldier is from the Albany Zouave Cadets, Company A, 10th Regiment, New York State Militia, which became Company A, 177th New York Volunteers, in November 1862. (Anthony Gero collection.)

The 13th Regiment, National Guard, State of New York, was from Brooklyn, and its gray fatigue uniform is seen in this carte de visite. Note the metal 13 on this soldier's cap. The unit was on active duty for three months in 1861, wearing this uniform. When the 13th Regiment returned to Brooklyn, it helped form the 87th New York Volunteer Infantry, known as the 13th Brooklyn or 13th War Regiment. (Roger Sturcke collection.)

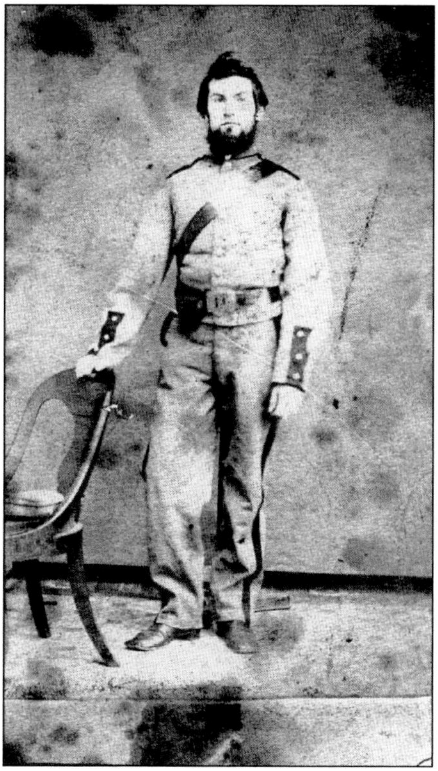

The 23rd Regiment, National Guard, State of New York, was a Brooklyn-based unit, organized in 1862 from the City Guard Reserve. The regiment went on active duty for one month, serving at Harrisburg, Pennsylvania, during the Gettysburg campaign. This carte de visite, with a photographer's mark of "Knapp's Gallery, 42 Street, Brooklyn," shows the 23rd Regiment in a gray dress similar to that of the 13th Regiment. (Roger Sturcke collection.)

This carte de visite is identified as Col. Jeremiah V. Meserole of the 47th Regiment, New York State Militia. The 47th Regiment was organized in Brooklyn in 1862 and was issued federal uniforms. Note the 47 on this officer's cap. Later on, a gray uniform, like that of the 23rd Regiment, was used by the 47th Regiment. The 47th Regiment was on active duty for short periods in 1862 and 1863. (Roger Sturcke collection.)

The 51st Regiment, National Guard, State of New York, from Syracuse, was never called up for active duty by the federal government. As seen in this carte de visite, this soldier wears a combination of United States Infantry–style dress and a pre–Civil War waist belt. The 51st Regiment helped form the 12th Regiment, New York Volunteers, in 1861. The photographer's label for this image reads, "D M'Glashan's, No. 12 South Salina Street, Syracuse, N.Y." (Roger Sturcke collection.)

This carte de visite photograph is inscribed "Geo. Vanderhude, June 1863." Regimental documents show that Vanderhude was in Company C, 56th Regiment, National Guard, State of New York. His uniform is the "chasseur" pattern, with appropriate piping issued to the 56th Regiment in 1863. His kepi, with its New York shield plate and pom-pom, is clearly visible. The photographer is unknown. (Anthony Gero collection.)

With a photographer's mark of "John S. Shipman, Artist, 146 Court St., Amity, Brooklyn," this picture shows a National Guardsman who is also in the 56th Regiment. Under magnification, a 56 can be seen on his cap. His chasseur-patterned uniform is the same as seen in the previously presented Vanderhude image. Records indicate that only a few units received this chasseur pattern, the 56th Regiment being one of these. (Anthony Gero collection.)

This private served in Company H, 71st Regiment, National Guard, State of New York, around 1863–1865. He does not wear the M1863 polka jacket, but rather, an M1861 State of New York jacket with percussion cap pocket. This distinctive feature is visible by the watch chain hooked to his button. Note the company and regimental number on his cap, both made of metal. There is no photographer's backmark on this carte de visite. (Anthony Gero collection.)

An officer of the 84th Regiment, National Guard, State of New York, formed in June 1863 in New York City, poses in this carte de visite. Note the 84 on his cap. The regiment was called to active duty in Baltimore for 30 days in July 1863. The picture's photographer is identified as "Israel & Co, Baltimore Street, Baltimore." (Roger Sturcke collection.)

Taken in Maryland, this picture shows another officer of the 84th Regiment. Note his foot officer's sword and sash, which denote his rank. The photographer's backmark reads, "Israel & Co, Baltimore Street, Baltimore." By 1876, the regiment had disbanded. (Roger Sturcke collection.)

This image is inscribed "O. R. Wine." The soldier wears a distinctive National Guard kepi, which has a New York shield plate and pom-pom. Wine reportedly served in the 1st Brigade, 3rd Division, 2nd Army Corps, Army of the Potomac. Whether he wore this uniform while in federal service is not clear. The carte de visite's backmark is "A. Corden of Troy, N.Y." (Anthony Gero collection.)

Judging by his uniform and the style of his shako, this musician was in either the New York State Militia or National Guard, State of New York, around 1860–1870. The glare on the shako's plate obscures the number of the unit to which he was attached. The carte de visite's photographer is identified as "Weldbillig, Hudson Ave. and S. Pearl St., Albany, N.Y." (Anthony Gero collection.)

Labeled as "Pvt E. S. Covell 4th Co 7th Regt," this private wears the 7th Regiment's National Guard, State of New York, short-lived gray chasseur uniform trimmed with black, and black shako with green plumage. Never popular, this uniform was worn only between 1865 and 1868 and abandoned when the gray and black tailed uniforms were revived. This carte de visite has a photographer's mark of "G. W. Loud., 132 Bowery, New York." (Anthony Gero collection.)

Two

Triumphant Times 1870–1897

Adopting the name Yates Dragoons, honoring Syracuse clothing manufacturer Alonzo C. Yates, in 1872, Separate Troop of Cavalry C, National Guard, State of New York, wore a variety of old and new cavalry dress. In this carte de visite, which notes the photographer as "John Austen, 60 South Salina Street, Syracuse," the officer is documented wearing an 1830s-to-1840s-style light dragoon helmet, with a helmet plate displaying *YD*. The headgear is adorned with white horsehair and has a red stand-up plume. By 1881, the troop was converted to artillery and in the 1890s was designated the 5th Battery. (Anthony Gero collection.)

Separate Troop of Cavalry M, from Utica, was described as wearing a dark blue frock coat trimmed with yellow facings in the *1879 Adjutant General's Inspection Report*. This photograph adds additional data not mentioned in the report (especially the troop's Prussian-style helmet) and shows the value of supportive photographic evidence. The photographer's label of this cabinet image reads, "Thomas & Bartlett, Genesee & Fayette, Utica, N.Y." (Anthony Gero collection.)

A sergeant of the National Guard, State of New York, probably of Battery B, stands in full-dress uniform. According to the *1879 Adjutant General's Inspection Report*, this battery was based in Brooklyn and wore a blue Prussian-style frock coat with red trim and black helmet with red plume. The carte de visite notes that "Fred Ulrick, 156 Bowery, N.Y." was the photographer and helps confirm the report's description of the battery's uniform. (Anthony Gero collection.)

This oval portrait shows a first lieutenant of the 5th Battery, 4th Brigade, National Guard, State of New York. Formed in Syracuse in 1881, this battery was in service until disbanded in 1897. Notice the battery's number inside gold-embroidered cross cannons on his dark blue chasseur cap. The cap's piping, his full-dress helmet cords across the breast of his coat, and the pads of his gold shoulder knots are all red. Also visible are several of his medals. (Anthony Gero collection.)

An enlisted man of the 6th Battery, National Guard, State of New York, around 1881–1885, wears the regulation double-breasted coat with red artillery trimmings. His cap has a metal insignia of crossed cannons with a 6 in the upper angle. His belt plate displays the characters *SNY*. The battery was from Binghamton, and this image has a mark of "Gilmer, 80 Court St.," a photographer in that city. (Anthony Gero collection.)

This is also a private of the 6th Battery, as seen by the metal numbers 6 on his coat's collar and the upper angle of the crossed cannons on his cap. His dark blue uniform is faced and trimmed with red, the artillery's branch of service color. He carries a mounted sword, as befits his status. The photograph was taken by Tupper of Binghamton. (Roger Sturcke collection.)

Pictured here is a corporal of the Signal Corps, 3rd Brigade, National Guard, State of New York, around 1881–1888. With his orange facings and red and white cloth signal flags inside his chevrons, this image shows the full-dress uniform. Although his helmet is not seen, its orange helmet cords are arranged according to style. On his collar is a metal 3 for the 3rd Brigade. The photographer's mark is "Pirie MacDonald, Albany, N.Y." (Anthony Gero collection.)

In this image, another corporal of the Signal Corps, 3rd Brigade, poses in an identical uniform as in the previous portrait. Note the yellow metal numeral 3 on the collar of the uniform, which, along with the orange facings, dates the portrait to 1881–1888. This cabinet photograph is also marked "Pirie MacDonald, Albany, N.Y." (Anthony Gero collection.)

This carte de visite of a drummer, 5th Regiment, National Guard, State of New York, has a photographer's label of "Schwind, 27 Avenue A, New York." He wears a distinctly blue Prussian-style full-dress coat with red trimmings, as confirmed in the *1879 Adjutant General's Inspection Report*. His "crows nests," the trimmings on the coat's shoulders, identify him as a musician. Visible on each shoulder straps is a 5. By 1882, the 5th Regiment was disbanded. (Anthony Gero collection.)

On the reverse of this cabinet image is written, "Col. Charles Spencer," who commanded the 5th Regiment of the National Guard, State of New York, around 1875–1879. In this pose, he shows off his engraved sword and his regiment's distinctive Prussian helmet with sunburst-style helmet plate. His officer's pattern *NY* belt plate is also visible. The photographer's mark is "Howell, New York." (Anthony Gero collection.)

An officer of the 7th Regiment, National Guard, State of New York, poses in full dress, in the regiment's traditional gray and black tailed uniform. The shako was worn by the regiment in the 1870s and early 1880s in all seasons, before a helmet was adopted for summer use. Note the 7 on the shako plate and the *NY* on the belt plate. The picture has a photographer's mark of "J. Ludovici, 899 Broadway." (Anthony Gero collection.)

A private in full-dress marching order of Company G, 7th Regiment, poses in this cabinet image. His epaulets are white-fringed with black tops. Notice how his overcoat is rolled up on his knapsack. This style of the soldier's dress dates the image to somewhere between 1875 and 1888. The photographer's label reads, "M. Goldstein, Artist and photographer, 1000 Third Ave., NY." (Roger Sturcke collection.)

This cabinet image shows a private of Company F, 7th Regiment, in full-dress uniform, around 1870–1885. The uniform is set off by the striking white body belt and shoulder belt with a large breastplate bearing a 7 on it. His shako's pom-pom is white. The photographer is identified as "James A. Bostwick, No 98 Sixth Ave, N.Y." (Anthony Gero collection.)

This private's image, by a Newark, New Jersey, photographer, shows the full-dress uniform of the 7th Regiment but also helps verify the regiment's forage cap worn in the 1875–1888 period. This decorated enlisted man is also in Company G, as seen by the letter on his belt plate. (Roger Sturcke collection.)

This sergeant's image from the 7th Regiment is marked "July 1884" on the reverse and helps document the regimental dress worn in that decade. Also visible is his noncommissioned officer's sword carried on a white belt and leather frog. The painted backdrop in this cabinet image, which has a photographer's label of "Anderson, 785 Broadway, N.Y.," adds a military flare to the photograph. (Roger Sturcke collection.)

In this postcard snapshot, a private of Company E, 7th Regiment, stands outside his tent around 1880–1890. The image shows his regiment's gray nine-button undress coat with black cuffs, shoulder straps, and collar. He wears white trousers, so one can assume the photograph was taken during the summer months, when white trousers were allowed. (Anthony Gero collection.)

This carte de visite, dated around 1870–1872, shows the flamboyant tycoon James Fisk Jr. in the blue full-dress uniform of the 9th Regiment, National Guard, State of New York. Notice his regimental shako plate, red heron plume, and gold baldric belt. Fisk, who became colonel on April 7, 1870, was killed on January 6, 1872. The image has a photographer's label of "Photograph Novelty" but does not list a place of business. (Roger Sturcke collection.)

Standing proudly in his blue full-dress uniform, with red and gold trim, this company-grade officer of the 9th Regiment shows some panache in this cabinet photograph from around 1876–1881. Note the flowing red cock-feathered plume on his black shako, as mentioned in the *1879 Adjutant General's Inspection Report*. The officer's *NY* belt plate can be clearly seen. (Roger Sturcke collection.)

A first sergeant of Company H, 9th Regiment, sits for his portrait in his blue full-dress uniform around 1881–1888. Note the number 9 on his breastplate and helmet's plate. His five lengths of service stripes in gold braid, along with his gold sergeant's chevrons, stand out. The photographer is identified as "De Youngs, 815 Broadway, N.Y." (Anthony Gero collection.)

Officers of the 9th Regiment are pictured around 1881–1884; on the back is written "Co F, 9th Regt Peekskill Ist Lt. Haute [?] Capt. Walton 2nd Lt. Marko [?]." These officers wear full-dress uniforms, but the white trousers and New York–pattern helmets indicate that the image was probably taken in the summer. (Anthony Gero collection.)

A corporal of Company B, 10th Regiment, National Guard, State of New York, is shown about 1870–1877. The corporal wears a "walking out dress"—a gray tailed full-dress coat, with black trim, white epaulets, and a pillbox cap. The company was called the Washington Continentals, and the letters *WC* are embroidered on the pillbox cap. The 10th Regiment was an Albany-based unit, but this image was by Powers at 225 State Street, Schenectady. (Anthony Gero collection.)

When the old 10th Regiment was reduced in 1881, a new battalion called the 10th Separate Battalion was formed in the Albany area. It is noted that this sergeant, dressed in the new 1881-pattern, double-breasted blue state uniform, trimmed in light blue, was photographed by "Malone of Albany, N.Y. & Troy, N.Y." Note this corporal's pillbox cap positioned on the ground. (Anthony Gero collection.)

On the reverse of this cabinet image is written, "Maj. Arthur T. Hills M.D. Surgeon 12th Infantry N.G. S.N.Y." Major Hills wears his regimental full-dress uniform, which, according to the *1879 Adjutant General's Inspection Report*, was a dark blue dress coat with light blue facings and large gold-bullion epaulets. He also has a straight hilted, medical staff officer's sword. Staff officers wore a blue shako with gold trim. (Roger Sturcke collection.)

This is another officer of the 12th Regiment, around 1876–1881. His status as a staff officer is denoted by the large white shako plume, shoulder belt, and sword style. His dress uniform is trimmed with gold lace, as documented in the *1879 Adjutant General's Inspection Report*. The portrait identifies "Rockwood & Co., 845 Broadway, N.Y." as the photographer. (Anthony Gero collection.)

This officer of the 12th Regiment wears the blue undress coat with black trim and buttons, around 1881–1894. His forage cap has the large-size officer's insignia that could be worn in the early part of the 1880s. On the reverse is written, "Wm F Catterfield," who may be the individual seen here. "James H. Stead, 583 6th Ave., N.Y." is cited as the photographer. (Roger Sturcke collection.)

This cabinet image, which identifies the photographer as "J. K. Cole, 174 Sixth Avenue, New York," shows an officer of the 13th Regiment, National Guard, State of New York, about 1876–1888. Note the officer-style insignia on his blue forage cap. His blue coat, gold shoulder knots, gold leather sword belt with an *NY* belt plate, and white gloves complete his uniform. (Roger Sturcke collection.)

Here stands a private of the 13th Regiment, wearing old and new uniform apparel between 1881 and 1887. He wears a dark blue double-breasted M1881 New York State dress coat with light blue trim with an old-style white regimental shoulder belt and breastplate from the 1870s, when the 13th Regiment wore a gray dress uniform, trimmed in black. The photographer's label reads, "JW Crawford, 543 Fulton Street, Brooklyn." (Anthony Gero collection.)

This cabinet image is of an officer in the 14th Regiment, National Guard, State of New York, sometime between 1890 and 1900. He is in a newer-style undress coat with black trim. His regimental and state affiliations are embroidered in gold upon the collar of this uniform. The 14th Regiment was a famous unit that was based in Brooklyn and served in the Civil War as the 84th New York Volunteer Infantry. (Roger Sturcke collection.)

This large composite portrait is of the 21st Regiment, National Guard, State of New York, prior to its disbanding in 1881–1882. It shows its full-dress uniforms, which were dark blue tailed coats with infantry trimmings and white epaulets, according to the *1879 Adjutant General's Inspection Report*. The image's label reads, "Presented to Capt H. Haubennestel by Co G, 21st Reg't, NG, SNY Dec 22 '81." This regiment was based in Poughkeepsie. (Anthony Gero collection.)

In this c. 1876 photograph, a private of the 22nd Regiment, National Guard, State of New York, stands in his white dress uniform with blue facings. The regiment's dress was patterned after the style of the Austrian army. His black shako has a New York shield plate with regimental number. His belt plate shows the letters *SNY* and is worn with a black belt. The image was taken by a New York City artisan at 815 Broadway. (Roger Sturcke collection.)

This cabinet image's reverse is inscribed, "Compliments of Geo W Brown. Drum Major 22nd Regt N.G. S.N.Y. 1885." Note the regimental number 22 on his belt plate. The famous white dress of the regiment is depicted here in stunning detail. The photographer is listed as "Dana, 14th St & 6th Avenue, New York." (Anthony Gero collection.)

This group photograph shows officers and men of the 22nd Regiment, based in New York City, wearing their white full-dress coats, trimmed with light blue. Between 1881 and 1884, the regiment adopted English-pattern dress helmets to replace its French-style shakos. Gold dress chevrons, adopted by the U.S. Regular Army in 1888 and worn by the National Guard, State of New York, are visible on the sergeant on the left. The distinctive Remington rifles used in New York State prior to 1897 are noticeable as well. (Anthony Gero collection.)

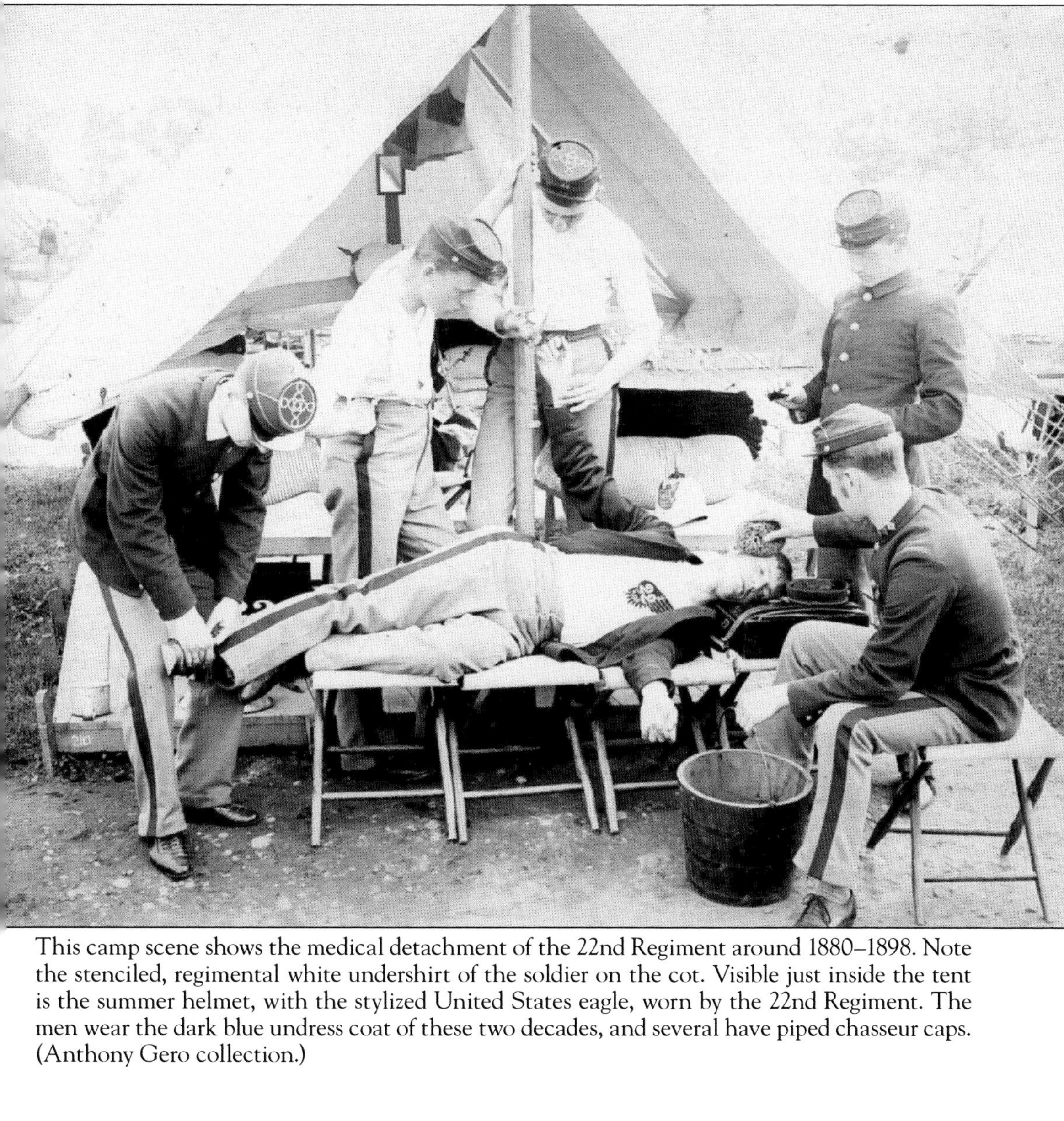

This camp scene shows the medical detachment of the 22nd Regiment around 1880–1898. Note the stenciled, regimental white undershirt of the soldier on the cot. Visible just inside the tent is the summer helmet, with the stylized United States eagle, worn by the 22nd Regiment. The men wear the dark blue undress coat of these two decades, and several have piped chasseur caps. (Anthony Gero collection.)

In this carte de visite, a private of Company F, 23rd Regiment, National Guard, State of New York, stands for his portrait in the unit's gray and black full-dress uniform around 1869–1881. His uniform is described in the *1879 Adjutant General's Inspection Report.* His belt plate is a Greek cross of regimental pattern. According to the back of this image, the picture was taken by "Rawson, New Gallery, 255 and 257 Fulton, opposite Clinton, Brooklyn." (Anthony Gero collection.)

This image is identified as "Chaplain Sam DeWater, 23rd Regt, N.Y.N.G.," taken by "Alava Pearsall, Fulton and Flatbush Ave, Brooklyn, N.Y." Note the State of New York–embroidered shield device on his black staff officer's dress hat. His uniform is black, with plain black buttons. His chaplain's shoulder straps can be seen in this image as well. (Anthony Gero collection.)

This cabinet image shows an unidentified sergeant of Company A, probably from the 25th Regiment, National Guard, State of New York, an Albany-based unit. He wears a gray dress uniform with black trim and gray-striped black trousers. By 1881, the 25th Regiment was disbanded. The photographer is noted as "MacDonalds, Bleecker Hall, 519 Broadway, Albany." (Anthony Gero collection.)

A sergeant identified on the image as "Sarg W S Crane D Co 44th Regt N.G.S.N.Y." poses for his picture in his full-dress uniform around 1872–1879. Notice his New York State–style shako and his breastplate, where the number 44 is visible. The coat's cuff slashes are highly unusual for this era. By 1877, the 44th Regiment, from the Binghamton area, was disbanded. (Anthony Gero collection.)

The dark blue background pads on this company-grade officer's gold-braided shoulder knots and the style of his helmet date this image to sometime between 1881 and 1888. The cabinet photograph shows an officer of the 47th Regiment (Brooklyn), National Guard, State of New York, in his full-dress winter uniform, with black dress helmet. It was taken by Duryea of Brooklyn. (Roger Sturcke collection.)

A private of Company E, 47th Regiment, is seen in this cabinet image, which has a photographer's label that reads, "William Jessen, 2601 & 2603 Atlantic Ave, 26th Ward, Brooklyn." On the reverse is written, "your friend P. F. Crane Brooklyn N.Y." The image dates to sometime between 1884 to 1892, as indicated by the double-breasted style of the coat and the regimental insignia. (Roger Sturcke collection.)

A private of Company A, 47th Regiment, is dressed in his garrison, or fatigue, uniform. He wears a variety of transitional clothing—an M1895 cap, new-pattern sack coat without piping, and dark blue web cartridge belt with a distinctive *H* belt plate for the 45/70 Springfield Trapdoor rifle. The photographer's mark of this cabinet image is "Hoffmann, 803 Broadway, Brooklyn, N.Y." (Anthony Gero collection.)

A private of Company K, 49th Regiment, National Guard, State of New York, poses in his gray tailed dress coat, which is trimmed in black, around 1872–1881. Note the New York shield plate with regimental number on his gray cloth kepi. His cap's pom-pom is black, as is confirmed by the *1879 Adjutant General's Inspection Report*. The 49th Regiment was based in Cayuga County, but Company K was from Seneca County. The photographer is identified as "A. H. Parker, Seneca Falls, N.Y." (Anthony Gero collection.)

Members of the prizewinning team of the 51st Regiment, National Guard, State of New York, gather for a photograph, taken at Creedmor in 1879. Observe their variety of full-dress and undress uniforms. The 51st Regiment was headquartered in Syracuse and drew its companies from Onondaga County. Between 1881 and 1884, the regiment was disbanded. (Anthony Gero collection.)

An officer of the 54th Regiment, National Guard, State of New York, poses in this image. Notice the circle device on his coat sleeve, which may be a brevet-rank badge awarded to those who achieved higher rank in the Civil War. Based in Rochester (Monroe County), the 54th Regiment disbanded in 1881. This image has a label of "Photo by Gadfrey, Rochester, N.Y. Sunbeam Gallery, 81 E. Main Street." (Roger Sturcke collection.)

Showing the dark blue undress uniform worn by New York officers from 1881 to 1892, an officer poses for this cabinet image. On his kepi, the number 65 is embroidered above crossed rifles, which documents his membership in the 65th Regiment, National Guard, State of New York, a Buffalo-based unit. Additionally, on the reverse is written, "May 1889." The photographer's frontmark is "Leo Palmer, 512 Main Street Buffalo, N.Y." (Anthony Gero collection.)

On the reverse of this cabinet image is written, "Compliments of W. J. Parsons Capt 65th Regt N.Y.S. Buffalo NY Commanding Co H." Captain Parsons's dress conforms to the period of 1881–1892, especially when the style and color of his shoulder knot are taken into account. According to the photograph, it was taken by "Bellsmith Bros, 446 Main St, Opp. German Ins. Building, Buffalo, N.Y." (Anthony Gero collection.)

In this large albumen print, several members of the 65th Regiment are seen in camp, along with their civilian guests. Notice the stenciled 65 on some of the soldiers' felt hats. The image dates from the 1890s or early 1900s. (Roger Sturcke collection.)

A private of Company K, 69th Regiment, National Guard, State of New York, poses around 1897–1898, wearing his five-button sack coat, piped on the collar with white, which was the infantry's branch color. This style of piping was worn by all New York units at the time. His trousers appear to be of brown, or a similarly drab color. He wears an *NY* belt plate on a dark blue web belt. The portrait was taken by Kempf's Photo Studio. (Anthony Gero collection.)

A private poses in the dark blue full-dress uniform of the 71st Regiment, National Guard, State of New York, worn between 1871 and 1881. His belt plate identifies him as a member of Company C, and his regimental number appears inside his shako's plate. This cabinet image has a photographer's label of "Fredrick's, Broadway and 9th St., N.Y." (Roger Sturcke collection.)

The officer here is probably from the 71st Regiment prior to 1881, when this style of dark blue tailed coat was worn. His gold-embroidered baldric belt is visible in great detail. The oak leaf on his gold-bullion epaulets denote his rank. The image is marked "H. Greer Photographer, 256 Bowery, N.Y." (Anthony Gero collection.)

This staff officer is from the National Guard, State of New York, around 1871–1881; note his *NY* belt plate. His uniform, which appears to be a dark blue tailed coat, could be from the 71st Regiment, but his shako's plate is obscured by plumage. The photographer's mark reads, "S. A. Taylor, 977 Fulton Street, Brooklyn." (Anthony Gero collection.)

A private of Company C, 71st Regiment, is pictured around 1881–1884, wearing white trousers with a white summer helmet that does not have a New York–style helmet plate but a United States–pattern eagle plate instead. His coat cuffs and collar are light blue. Additionally, he wears Civil War–style brass shoulder scales worn by some units in the 1880s. The photographer is listed as "R. A. Lewis, 190 Park Row, New York." (Anthony Gero collection.)

An officer in the 71st Regiment wears the rarely photographed pillbox cap used by some units between 1875 and 1900. The dark blue cap has a metal device of crossed rifles and a 71 on it. His dark blue undress coat, with black trim and buttons, dates to before 1894. The photographer's label is "S. A. Taylor, 277 Fulton Street, Brooklyn, New York." (Anthony Gero collection.)

A private in the 71st Regiment, around 1897–1900, shows the thrift in use of military apparel. He wears a mixture of uniform styles, such as old blue trousers with a white stripe, the new drab coat, and a dark blue web belt with *NY* belt plate. His drab hat is stenciled with a 71. The image is marked as taken by "Sinn." (Anthony Gero collection.)

This tintype features an unidentified private, Company B, 74th Regiment, National Guard, State of New York (Buffalo), around 1879–1881. According to the *1879 Adjutant General's Inspection Report*, the 74th Regiment's rank and file wore a gray dress uniform, trimmed with black, white epaulets, and a black shako with a white pom-pom. The image shows how important photographic evidence is in documenting written accounts of military uniforms. (Anthony Gero collection.)

This cabinet image has a reverse notation of "George Sheldon Co H 74 Regt," as taken by "Bellswith Bros, 446 Main St, Buffalo, N.Y." Due to the style of his coat's cuff lace and the regimental crest on the helmet, the picture dates from the period between 1876 and 1881. It was not unusual for officers in this period to wear different color uniforms from their men. (Roger Sturcke collection.)

This large albumen print is labeled on the reverse, "Comp H 1893 Peekskill NY 74th NG SNY." Upon examination of their dress and insignia, these soldiers' uniforms conform to that year. Note the Remington rifles stacked on each side of the group. The company's drummer sits with his instrument on the ground on the right side, while the company's bugler sits on the left. (Roger Sturcke collection.)

This large print is marked on the reverse, "74th Regiment N. G. N.Y. Buffalo, N.Y. Col. Fox seated in center." The image can be dated to 1891–1894, based upon the style of undress coats worn. The seated officer second from the left wears a full-dress uniform, but with summer cork helmet that is stenciled with a 74. (Roger Sturcke collection.)

Senior noncommissioned officers are posing in this large albumen print. On the back is written, "74th Regiment Buffalo N.Y. Standing Theodore B Sheldon 3rd from left Frank Wood Argus 5th Curtis During 7th." These noncommissioned sergeants wear officer-style cap devices and carry swords, as befits their high enlisted man's rank. The image dates to 1892–1898. (Roger Sturcke collection.)

A possible member of the 1st Separate Company (Fenton Guards), 31st Brigade, National Guard, State of New York, organized in 1875 at Jamestown, appears here. Made up of Swedish Americans, the company patterned its dress on the Swedish colors, blue and yellow. Note the 1 on his belt plate. In 1877, the company's designation was changed to the 4th Separate Company. This carte de visite was taken by a Jamestown photographer. (Anthony Gero collection.)

Identified as "G.W. Nellis," as photographed by "Squyer, No 130 Genesee Street, Auburn, N.Y.," this cabinet image shows a member of the 2nd Separate Company, National Guard, State of New York. Formed in 1881, the company took the honorary name of Wheeler Rifles, after Mayor Cyrenus Wheeler Jr., and became one of the premier companies in the state by 1885. The style of collar insignia dates the image to 1881–1884. (Anthony Gero collection.)

This albumen prints shows 10 identified members of the 2nd Separate Company, around 1881–1888. A variety of winter and summer full-dress uniforms, along with fatigue uniforms, are highlighted in this military tableau. Note how the chevrons are placed on the overcoat, as seen by the noncommissioned officer standing on the left. The seated officer in the middle is Capt. William M. Kirby, a Civil War veteran. The 2nd Separate Company was formed in 1881 when the local 49th Regiment was disbanded and reorganized into this separate company. (Collection of the Cayuga Museum.)

Identified as "First Lieut. Frank H. Griswold," this officer of the 2nd Separate Company shows a brevet-rank insignia on the collar of his full-dress uniform. If an individual achieved a higher rank in the Civil War, he was allowed, by New York State regulations, to wear that rank upon the collar of his dress uniform. (Collection of the Cayuga Museum.)

Taken at the memorial dedication of the 1st Independent Battery, New York Volunteers, on July 3, 1887, this image shows the survivors of Cowan's Battery from the Civil War. In the background, the 2nd Separate Company stands in formation in its summer uniforms, near the spot where part of Pickett's Charge was stopped by the 1st Independent Battery. The memorial still stands at Gettysburg. (Anthony Gero collection.)

Due to the style of his coat with its light blue facings, this man can be identified as a soldier of the 3rd Separate Company, National Guard, State of New York, around 1881–1884. The photographer's mark, "Young of Oneonta, N.Y.," helps confirm this since the 3rd Separate Company was based in that city. Note the Remington 50/70 caliber rolling block rifle, New York State's standard weapon until 1897. (Anthony Gero collection.)

Another private of the 3rd Separate Company is shown here. Written on the reverse is "F. H. Roundy 1896." After 1892, the coat's piping would be white for the infantry. The collar devices are marksmanship awards. What makes the image unusual is the private's Merriam pack, which was not adopted by New York until around 1897; perhaps this company was field-testing the pack before then. The photographer of this cabinet image is identified as "Patten, Oneonta, N.Y." (Anthony Gero collection.)

Re-formed in 1876, the Troy Citizens Corps in 1877 was designated the 6th Separate Company of Infantry, National Guard, State of New York. Adopting a full-dress uniform of a red frock coat with blue facings, gold trimming, and metal shoulder scales, it became one of the state's elite companies. This cabinet image shows the 6th Separate Company's dress uniform around 1877–1883 with the unit's distinctly Prussian-style helmet. (Anthony Gero collection.)

Another private of the 6th Separate Company, around 1877–1883, sits for his portrait in this cabinet image. Although he does not wear his full-dress helmet, his distinctive, red full-dress uniform is seen, along with his white crossed belts and large cross belt plate. The photographer's mark is "Fisk & Reitmeyer, Troy, N.Y." (Anthony Gero collection.)

On the back of this large albumen print is written, "TCC 6th Sep Co Buffalo Strike 1892." TCC stands for Troy Citizen Corps. Note the two company guidons, carried by members standing at the top of the group. The men are shown in field order as befits their duty in Buffalo. Several of the officers have rolled their overcoats over their shoulders. Officers and men wear the standard blue New York State fatigue dress of that period. (Anthony Gero collection.)

This cabinet image is identified on the reverse as "F. D. Rankin, 8th Sep Co. N.G.S.N.Y. Rochester N.Y." His dress conforms to the National Guard, State of New York, styles in the 1884–1890 period. The photographer is noted as "W. J. Lee, 62 State Street, Rochester, N.Y." The 8th Separate Company was formed when the Rochester-based 54th Regiment was reduced to several separate companies in 1881. (Anthony Gero collection.)

This is 1st Lt. Frederick W. G. Bailey of the 8th Separate Company, National Guard, State of New York, pictured around 1891–1898. Around his neck, he wears a New York Faithful Service Medal, not to be confused with the United States Medal of Honor. In 1878, Bailey started in the 54th Regiment and retired from the guard in 1902. The photographer's label reads, "Ranger & Whitmore, 30 East Main Street, Rochester, N.Y." (Anthony Gero collection.)

Standing in his full-dress uniform with winter helmet, a private of the 11th Separate Company, National Guard, State of New York, from Mount Vernon, poses here. The style of his dress suggests a estimated date of 1881–1888. Note his Remington rifle, with its distinctive profile. The picture has a photographer's mark of "Stivers, 56 Fourth Avenue, Mt. Vernon, N.Y." (Roger Sturcke collection.)

The 11th Separate Company is visible in this outdoor photograph. The men wear white summer trousers with their dark blue coats. Based upon the seated officers, and the style of enlisted men's cap and insignia, the image dates to 1881–1892. Note the two company drummers. The box-style knapsack was used in New York until 1897, when replaced by the Merriam packs. (Anthony Gero collection.)

This officer is probably of the 12th Separate Company of Troy, National Guard, State of New York. The image can be dated to 1892–1898, since the pads on his gold-embroidered shoulder knots appear to be white, which was the infantry branch color of that time. The number 12 appears on each pad also. The photographer is identified as "Brusie & Boice, River & Fourth Sts, Troy, N.Y." (Roger Sturcke collection.)

This cabinet image, which has a photographer's mark reading "Laidler 11 East Third St, Jamestown, N.Y.," shows a private of the 13th Separate Company (Fenton Guards), National Guard, State of New York, formed in 1875 as the 1st Separate Company. After a fire destroyed its old uniforms, new ones of blue and yellow were adopted, to again reflect the company's Swedish heritage. Note this soldier's script *SNY* belt plate. He stands before a painted backdrop. (Anthony Gero collection.)

This carte de visite shows a private of the 14th Separate Company, National Guard, State of New York. According to the *1879 Adjutant General's Inspection Report*, the company, based in Batavia, wore a dark blue dress coat, with light blue and gold trimmings and sky blue trousers. Since this image lists "C. W. Tallman, 80 & 82 Main Street, Batavia, N.Y." as the photographer, this soldier is probably in the 14th Company. After 1879, the company was disbanded. (Anthony Gero collection.)

This portrait shows a private in the 15th Separate Company, National Guard, State of New York, wearing a gray, black-trimmed, tailed full-dress coat before 1881. The New York State–pattern staff buttons are clearly visible on his coat. The photographer's mark reads, "F. B. Clench, 39 & 41 East Avenue, Lockport, N.Y." (Anthony Gero collection.)

Members of the 15th Separate Company, Lockport, pose in their state-issued fatigue uniforms, around 1881–1892. The trouser stripe seen on some of their clothing is dark blue, which dates the image to these years. Between 1892 and 1894, New York changed its infantry branch color to white. Additionally, several men wear white trousers, which were allowed in the summer months. (Roger Sturcke collection.)

This large prints shows the 18th Separate Company, National Guard, State of New York, from Glen Falls lined up before the photographer's lens. From the style of their dress uniforms and trouser stripes, which appear to be white, the image can be identified as having been taken between 1892 and 1897. Officers and men wear gaiters of a light color to protect their uniforms from wear while on the march. (Roger Sturcke collection.)

Organized in 1877, the Tibbet Cadets of Troy were designated the 21st Separate Company, 5th Brigade, 3rd Division, National Guard, State of New York, in 1878. On this cabinet image's reverse is written, "Yours . . . P. J. Carmichael 1879." He is likely the 21st Separate Company's member seen here in the company's blue dress uniform. Note the stylized *TC* insignia on his breastplate and forage cap. The photographer is identified as "Atkinson, Troy, N.Y." (Anthony Gero collection.)

Sometime in the 1880s, members of the Tibbet Cadets (the 21st Separate Company) changed their full dress to a black-trimmed gray coat and a gray dress helmet with white flowing plume. This cabinet image, with a photographer's mark that reads, "Lloyd of Troy, N.Y.," documents this new uniform and shows the élan of the company. Observe the *TC* collar badges, belt plate, and special-patterned helmet plate. (Anthony Gero collection.)

Members of the 22nd Separate Company, National Guard, State of New York, wore bearskin hats with their gray, black-trimmed full-dress uniforms prior to 1881–1882. As seen in this cabinet image, which has a photographer's label of "H. G. Brown, 400 Broadway, Saratoga, N.Y.," this corporal wears white trousers, indicating summer dress. As he poses in parade rest position, his Remington 50/70 caliber rifle is prominently seen. Note the painted backdrop in this photograph. (Anthony Gero collection.)

This corporal in the 22nd Separate Company shows off his new-pattern black winter helmet with New York–style helmet plate that has a 22 on it. His chevrons appear to be the M1888 gold pattern, which indicates a time frame of 1888–1890. This image notes "Epler & Arnold, Successor E. A. Record, Saratoga, N.Y." as the photographer. (Anthony Gero collection.)

This sergeant wears a five-button, plain sack coat without the typical New York–style, white piping on the collar. His chevrons appear to be white cloth, and on his dark blue forage cap is a metal number 22. The photographer is listed as "E. A. Record, Saratoga, N.Y.," and this image could date from between 1892 and 1894. (Anthony Gero collection.)

An officer in the 23rd Separate Company, National Guard, State of New York, from Hudson, poses in this cabinet portrait. On his coat, he wears a Civil War medal. The other device is a type of National Guard service medal. His uniform and forage cap date from approximately 1881 to 1890. (Anthony Gero collection.)

Gray uniforms were popular in New York in the 1870s and 1880s. In 1879, the 25th Separate Company, National Guard, State of New York, in Canandaigua wore a gray chasseur sack coat, trimmed and faced with black, as documented in the *1879 Adjutant General's Inspection Report*. This carte de visite by H. M. Finley of Canandaigua shows this style of dress. Visible on his black shako is a 25. Between 1881 and 1884, the company adopted the blue M1881 New York State uniform. (Anthony Gero collection.)

A 25th Separate Company unidentified private, from around 1885–1892, is shown here wearing the M1881 New York State coat with light blue facings. His buttons are New York State–staff pattern. His body belt appears to be white, but the belt plate is not clearly seen. The 25th Separate Company was based in Canandaigua from 1879 to 1892. The photographer's mark reads, "Crandall Bros, Canandaigua, N.Y." (Anthony Gero collection.)

These three enlisted men are from the 27th Separate Company, National Guard, State of New York, which was based in Malone. They wear the distinctive five-button, dark blue coat, piped with white on the collar, which helps identify them in New York's armed forces. Their *SNY* belt plates and 27 on their forage caps help to date the image to around 1892–1898. The photographer is identified as "Spencer, Malone, N.Y." (Anthony Gero collection.)

The 29th Separate Company, National Guard, State of New York (Oswego), was created when the 48th Regiment (Infantry) was disbanded in 1881. The African American civilian on the right is not a company member, since New York State did not allow African Americans in the guard from 1870 until 1915. The 29th Separate Company was consolidated with the 38th Separate Company (Oswego) to form the 48th Separate Company in 1892. (Anthony Gero collection.)

This photograph shows a member of the 30th Separate Company, National Guard, State of New York, in the full-dress uniform of 1899–1902. It was a single-breasted blue coat with white collar, shoulder straps, and piping. Since the 30th Separate Company was based in Elmira, the photographer, marked as "McFarlin, Elmira, N.Y.," helps document the unit as well. Note the soldier's medals on his chest. (Roger Sturcke collection.)

In this scene, members of the 30th Separate Company lounge, probably at Peekskill during their state camp. The company designation is marked on their Merriam packs. On the beds, their full-dress uniforms and helmets lay for inspection. The men wear two different styles of fatigue headgear allowed between 1892 and 1900. One is the forage cap, and the other is the recently adopted drab hat. (Anthony Gero collection.)

This postcard view shows the 34th Separate Company, National Guard, State of New York, and is marked "on field Day, Willard, N.Y." The 34th Separate Company was based in Geneva. Close inspection of the uniforms reveals that the image likely dates from the late 1890s to 1910. (Anthony Gero collection.)

This cabinet photograph shows an officer of the 37th Separate Company, National Guard, State of New York, from Schenectady in his gray, tailed full-dress coat, but wearing his dark blue forage cap with an *NY* logo. His attire represents "walking out" dress for the time period of 1879–1884. The photographer's label reads, "Burgess, Schenectady, N.Y." (Anthony Gero collection.)

Another company officer is shown here, from the 37th Separate Company. He wears an undress coat with black frogging, worn prior to 1894. His shoulder bars appear to be gold-trimmed with white facings. These elements of his dress suggest the transitional period in uniform styles from 1892 to 1894. This photograph is marked "Walter Talbot Studio, 505 State St., Schenectady, N.Y." (Anthony Gero collection.)

A sergeant of the 39th Separate Company, National Guard, State of New York, from Watertown, poses sometime between 1892 and 1898. He wears the full-dress winter uniform, as is evident from his black New York–pattern helmet. The infantry branch colors were white between 1892 and 1898, although this soldier seems to wear the M1888 gold dress chevrons. His *SNY* belt plate is visible too. The photograph was taken by Gray Brothers, Watertown. (Anthony Gero collection.)

Members of the 39th Separate Company are depicted here, around 1897–1898, probably at camp in Peekskill. The seated sergeant on the left wears a full-dress uniform, but with a campaign hat. Their trouser stripes appear to be white. Notice the Merriam packs behind the sergeant marked with the company's designation. (Roger Sturcke collection.)

With a photographer's label of "Zalner, Niagara Falls, N.Y.," this cabinet photograph shows a private of the 42nd Separate Company, National Guard, State of New York, around 1890–1897. His coat's white facings, metal collar number, and forage cap insignia are from those years. The 42nd Separate Company was based in Niagara Falls at that time. (Anthony Gero collection.)

This cabinet photograph shows an enlisted man of the Utica Citizen Corps, the 44th Separate Company, National Guard, State of New York. He wears an overcoat over his dress uniform. The style of the uniform and the *SNY* belt plate date from between 1881 and 1892. The photographer's mark reads, "Harris & Greene, 230 Genesee St., Utica, N.Y." (Roger Sturcke collection.)

The photographer's mark on this cabinet image is "Van B. Wheaton, 30–32 E. Main Street, Amsterdam, N.Y.," and a member of the 46th Separate Company, National Guard, State of New York, of that city poses. The style of his sack coat, web belt, and belt plate date the image as having been taken between 1897 and 1898. Note how the soldier has individualized his campaign hat by taking his forage cap insignia and wearing it on his hat. (Anthony Gero collection.)

A bandsman of the 48th Separate Company, National Guard, State of New York, from Oswego, poses in his dress blue uniform, around 1892–1898. His facings, belting, helmet cords, and plume are white, but his pants are dark blue. Although his helmet's plate has a 29 on it, a 48th Separate Company band photograph in the Oswego armory shows this same musician similarly attired. The photographer is listed as "Shayes 23 & 25 West Bridge Street, Oswego, N.Y." (Anthony Gero collection.)

Maj. William M. Kirby, who had served in the 3rd New York Volunteer Artillery between 1862 and 1865, sat for this image after 1896. Major Kirby was formerly captain of the 2nd Separate Company (Auburn) in 1881 but had been promoted to a position of general inspector of rifle practice on January 1, 1897. Note the metal insignia on his undress coat and the flaming bomb signifying the Ordnance Department. (Collection of the Cayuga Museum.)

This staff officer, who is described as "Department of the Engineer-in Chief," was reportedly photographed in 1881. Observe his New York–style staff chapeau, his *NY* belt plate, and, under close magnification, his engineer-style buttons with a castle on each. His sleeve's cuff braid was discontinued by the U.S. Regular Army and various National Guards after 1881. The photographer's mark on this cabinet image reads, "Pearsall 298 Fulton Street Brooklyn." (Anthony Gero collection.)

This scene shows a variety of medical personnel, officers and enlisted, men from various regiments and separate companies—the 13th Regiment and the 10th, 19th, and 24th Separate Companies. On the reverse is written, "State Camp July 1892." Notice the white brassard with red cross on five of the men's coats. Several officers wear white summer trousers. (Roger Sturcke collection.)

In this camp scene, additional medical men from New York State are depicted. Notice the knapsack's marking of "Hospital Knapsack N.G. S.N.Y." One man wears the old Civil War–style brassard of a green chevron with caduceus centered on his coat's sleeve. Others wear the newer white brassard with red cross, which was adopted in the 1890s. On the reverse of the image is written, "State Camp July 1892." (Roger Sturcke collection.)

An officer of one of the oldest independent companies allowed in New York State is seen in this cabinet image. Posing here is an officer of New York City's Old Guard, wearing the white dress uniform of around 1880–1898. Additionally, he sports a dark blue undress pillbox cap with script OG embroidered on it. The photographer's mark reads, "Anderson, 785 Broadway." (Anthony Gero collection.)

The original caption of this albumen print identifies those Old Guard members who posed in 1889. Note their black bearskin hats on the ground. Additionally, New York State's segregation policy is demonstrated by the unidentified company servant on the left, in uniform but not allowed to be a soldier in the Old Guard or in any of New York State's official military organizations during those years. (Anthony Gero collection.)

This unidentified Zouave was photographed by "Pomeroy, 18 West Main St., Rochester, N.Y.," as listed on the reverse. Between 1870 and 1885, there is evidence that an independent company dressed in Zouave uniforms was active in that city. New York State had Zouave-dressed units in its National Guard between 1866 and 1876, but Zouave styles had faded from favor between 1880 and 1890. (Anthony Gero collection.)

This tintype, with no identifying marks, is of four men who could be from New York State; reportedly the photograph came from the Hudson Valley. The revival of Continental dress was popular in many state National Guards during the United States centennial of 1876. Syracuse had such a company uniformed in this style. (Anthony Gero collection.)

Three

Growing Pains 1898–1916

This postcard's caption states, "10th Battalion Leaving Albany May 1st for Spanish Am. War" and shows the battalion's parade down from the state capitol building to the railroad station. The 10th Battalion, National Guard, New York, helped form part of the 1st Regiment, New York Volunteers, and served in Hawaii doing garrison duty there. The 10th Battalion was an Albany-area unit. (Roger Sturcke collection.)

This cabinet card carries the photographer's label "Davery's, Honolulu, Hawaii" and shows a private of Company K, 1st New York Volunteers, sent to garrison the Hawaiian Islands in 1898. He wears a blue U.S. Regular Army–issued blouse that he has customized with a small metal *N* and *Y* on the collar's points. The image was probably taken in December 1898, just before the 1st New York Volunteers left for home. (Anthony Gero collection.)

This photograph documents the 2nd New York Volunteers in field order, around 1898. Note the metal 2 on several soldiers' drab-colored campaign hats. The man in the blue coat wears an *NY* belt plate, while another, with the stenciled haversack that bears his separate company markings, wears a double-breasted overcoat. The 21st Separate Company from Troy was assigned to the 2nd New York Volunteers. (Anthony Gero collection.)

The front of this image reads, "Waterford Boys 2nd Regt N.Y. Inf." The reverse is also inscribed: "1 Andrew Spears Co. B 2 Clarence Deavenport Co. B 3 Harry Perrin ditto Co. B 4 Bert Lambert ditto Co. B 5 Capt Mc Gaffin ditto Co. B 6 Harry Harrury Co. B 7 Harry E. Sherwin Co. A 8 Q. M. Scrgt Ross Co. B 9 Edward Cole. Co. D." (Anthony Gero collection.)

This photograph also shows a member of the 2nd Regiment, National Guard, New York, around 1899–1902. His regiment's number is indicated by the 2 stenciled on his campaign hat. He wears the new-pattern service blouse with two white cloth 6s, for 6th Separate Company (Troy). The 2nd Regiment was made a permanent part of the National Guard in New York between 1899 and 1902. (Anthony Gero collection.)

The front of this photograph is labeled "Pierce HQs C 3rd REGT." Research into the records reveal that a Harry C. Pierce, age 24, did enlist at Syracuse in the 3rd Regiment, New York Volunteers. He was eventually promoted from corporal in Company C to second lieutenant in June 1898. (Roger Sturcke collection.)

This soldier is identified as Sidney B. Williams, age 25, who enlisted at Syracuse in the 3rd Regiment, New York Volunteers. Note the markings on his haversack, which read, "41 Sep Co NYNG." The 41st Separate Company was based in Syracuse and helped form the 3rd Regiment in 1898. The image bears the handwritten notation "Camp Meade PA Sept 12." (Roger Sturcke collection.)

The 2nd Separate Company from Auburn, now designated as Company M, 3rd Regiment, New York Volunteers, lines up on May 1, 1898, in a street of that city. As the company stands, uniformed in marching order, civilians watch from their homes and the street. The 3rd Regiment was composed of separate companies of the National Guard, New York. (Collection of the Cayuga Museum.)

This print lists "Forest Stamp, 116 Baldwin, Elmira, N.Y." as the photographer and shows 16 identified officers, mostly in the 3rd New York Volunteers. Comparing them to other identified photographs, the most distinguishable are "4. W H Kirby Lt Col 3rd Regt NYV Inf." and "15. A.M. Hall Major 3rd Regt NYV Inf." Kirby was the former captain of the 2nd Separate Company (Auburn), and Hall was the former captain of the 48th Separate Company (Oswego). (Anthony Gero collection.)

These two officers of the 71st New York Volunteers, formed from the 71st Regiment, National Guard, New York, wear the new-pattern dark blue field-service blouse of 1898–1900. Note the M1895 garrison cap, with embroidered New York shield, and the officer-styled *NY* belt plate. Their light blue trousers are marked with a white stripe. The photographer's mark is "Davis & Sandford, 246 Fifth Avenue, New York." (Anthony Gero collection.)

Pvt. Adam Rutz has taken his campaign hat's insignia for the 3rd Regiment, New York Volunteers, Company K, and placed it on his sack coat. The image dates from around 1898–1899, since the 203rd Regiment was composed of various separate companies for the Spanish-American War, then disbanded. The front label is of a Rome-based photographer, and Rutz's name is inscribed on the back. (Anthony Gero collection.)

This is a member of Company E, 203rd New York Volunteers, around 1898. He is identifiable by the metal insignia on his campaign hat, along with the metal letters *NYV* on his coat. His 2nd Army Corps badge is also worn on his coat. The original image has been clipped, so the photographer's mark is only hinted at. (Anthony Gero collection.)

This cabinet image features a possible member of the 203rd New York Volunteers, around 1898. Under magnification, his campaign hat's insignia suggests this regimental affiliation. Note his 2nd Army Corps badge on his coat's collar. He holds an earlier model Springfield 47/70 Trapdoor rifle with triangular bayonet. His tan Mills cartridge belt has a C clasp closure. The photographer is identified as "GE Bacon, Rome, N.Y." (Anthony Gero collection.)

This postcard's caption reads, "Red Cross Corps" at Peekskill. Upon examination, one guardsman, the third standing from the left, wears a New York–style piped coat. He also carries a medical knife on his belt, which has an *NY* belt plate. Notice how the red cross device is worn on the overcoat of the soldier standing on the left. The image dates from the period between 1892 and 1900. (Anthony Gero collection.)

This is another postcard snapshot that shows National Guardsmen from New York at the State Camp at Peekskill around 1898. Observe the right-hand soldier's trouser striping, which designates him as a musician. Under magnification, the wooden barrels are stenciled "65th Regt. N.Y." (Roger Sturcke collection.)

This shows members of the 2nd Separate Company (Auburn) in the new M1899 state full-dress uniforms. Their white collars have cutout numbers, revealing the dark blue beneath, which replaced the metal numbers of 1892–1898. Several wear length-of-service sleeve stripes. Some show war stripes, indicating service in the Spanish-American War, when they were in Company M, 3rd Regiment, New York Volunteers. One, in the second row, on the right, is a medical corpsman. His uniform's facings are green, representing that service branch, while his armband is white with a red cross. (Anthony Gero collection.)

This group photograph shows members of the 32nd Separate Company from Hoosic Falls, around 1892–1898. They wear the *NY* belt plate on their dark blue web belts, and their blouses are piped on the collar, all indications of military styles during that period. Each wears the campaign hat with company insignia. Notice what may be the company mascot in front of these soldiers. (Anthony Gero collection.)

This postcard shows Sergeant Evans, 41st Separate Company (Syracuse), in his dress uniform. His helmet spike is just visible on the left. The uniform's facings are white, but the 41 is cut out to reveal the dark blue beneath, a distinctive feature of the M1899 uniform. His New York Faithful Service Medal is seen around his neck and should not be confused with the United States Medal of Honor. (Anthony Gero collection.)

This large cabinet image by Cooper and Mac (?) of Ogdensburg shows a private of the 40th Separate Company, also from Syracuse but organized in 1894. The 40th was assigned to the 4th Battalion, National Guard, New York, in 1899. The private wears the newer-pattern blouse, without piping, worn by New York's armed forces from 1900 to 1902. His buttons appear to be New York State–staff pattern. (Anthony Gero collection.)

The spirit of the Edwardian age, which World War I destroyed, can be viewed in this image of either the 47th Separate Company or the 47th Regiment of the National Guard, New York. In this picture, taken on June 8, 1902, at Peekskill, soldiers and friends lounge and frolic before the photographer's lens. The distinctive *NY* on their Mills belt plates and new-patterned blouses help date the image to 1902. (Anthony Gero collection.)

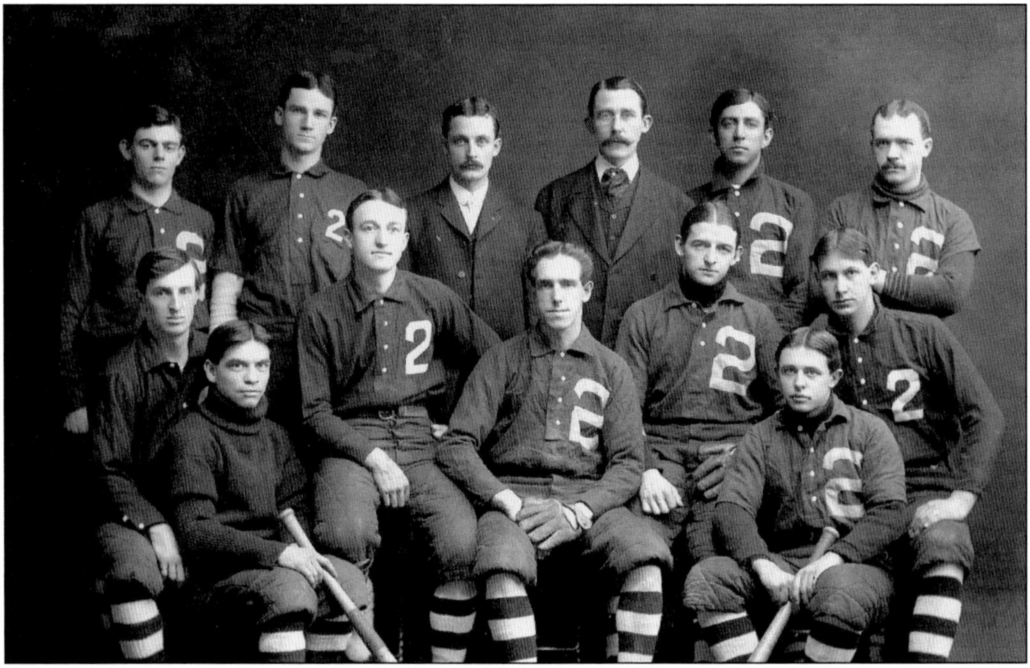

Baseball was popular in the U.S. Regular Army and state National Guards from 1861 to 1919. In this image titled "2d Sep.Co. 1904–1905," the company's indoor baseball team is depicted. Indoor baseball was played during the winter to keep the men in shape. By 1910, the company became Company M, 3rd Regiment. Federalized into the 108th Infantry in 1917, the company eventually fought in Europe. (Collection of the Cayuga Museum.)

This print is of an unidentified company, but because of the style of its full-dress uniforms, it can be dated around 1902–1904. Notice the cutout 2 on the enlisted men's collars, which suggests this is the 2nd Regiment, National Guard, New York. The infantry's facings at this time were white, and their caps are the M1902 style. The men appear to be outside their armory. (Anthony Gero collection.)

This image shows a sergeant of Company C, 3rd Regiment, National Guard, New York. Like the 2nd Regiment, the 3rd Regiment was made a permanent regiment in the National Guard, New York, between 1899 and 1902. He wears the M1899 dress coat but with the new-pattern 1902 dress hat. The infantry facings were still white. Notice how the discontinued helmet cords are worn with this uniform. (Anthony Gero collection.)

This group image is of members of the 7th Regiment, National Guard, New York, and is datable by the types of weapons stacked on the right. These are Krag rifles that replaced the Springfield 45/70 weapons of 1897–1901. The Krag rifles were used in New York's military forces between 1901 and 1908. Note the variety of summer and field dress these men wear. (Roger Sturcke collection.)

In 1896, the 23rd Regiment, National Guard, New York, underwent two uniform changes. First, its officers adopted a gray dress similar to that of the enlisted men; second, officers and men replaced their helmets with an Italian-style shako. Note the headgear's regimental plate, topped by a white plume. This image shows a staff officer in the 23rd Regiment's gray and black full-dress uniform worn until 1917. (Anthony Gero collection.)

This unidentified private is from Company G, 23rd Regiment, in the enlisted men's full-dress uniform. He also wears a white belt, breast cords, and gloves. His shako has the regimental number on its plate, and the shako's pom-pom is blue over white. The braiding on his coat is black, and his epaulets are white with black tops. (Anthony Gero collection.)

This postcard image shows the new drabness in field uniform colors adopted by the U.S. Regular Army and the various state National Guards around 1902–1904. Under magnification, this unidentified officer wears insignia of the 65th Regiment. Note the New York–style shield device embroidered on his cap. (Anthony Gero collection.)

On the reverse of this postcard is written, "HG Hicks Captain and Quartermaster 65th Regt N.G. N.Y. Camp Hughes Farmham, N.Y." In the *New York Adjutant General's Report of 1900*, a Howard Ogden Hicks is listed as a captain and quartermaster in the 65th Regiment. Notice the similarity of Hicks's uniform to the previous image. The image dates from the 1902–1904 period. (Anthony Gero collection.)

This large albumen print shows Company L, 13th Regiment, Heavy Artillery, National Guard, New York, around 1905 at Plum Island, as documented by the notation on the photograph. This regiment dates back to the old 13th New York State Militia from Brooklyn during the Civil War era. The men of Company L wear a variety of transitional dress, such as the dark blue web belts with *NY* belt plate for their Krag .30-caliber rifles, and drab uniforms. The seated officers have New York collar devices on their caps. Additionally, the enlisted men wear white gloves. (Anthony Gero collection.)

By 1906, the field dress of New York's military forces had gone modern, consisting of a drab uniform with little ornamentation. The notation on this postcard is "State Camp Peekskill June 1906," and it likely shows an infantry bugler holding his instrument. At that time, the infantry's branch color was light blue, so the bugle's cording would be of that color. (Anthony Gero collection.)

The handwritten notation on this postcard reads, "Camp Porter Farmham, N.Y. Aug, 1909 Faithfully Yours J.L. Baker." Note the medical patch this corpsman has stitched on his field shirt, just visible on his right sleeve, above the elbow. (Anthony Gero collection.)

The cap insignia of these two soldiers identifies them as belonging to Company A, 1st Regiment, National Guard, New York. The soldiers wear the newer-style dress uniform with light blue piping on their dark blue collars and shoulder straps. Additionally, they each have the metal letters *NY* on their coat collars. The image dates from the 1910–1916 period. (Anthony Gero collection.)

This photograph is of a sergeant from Company E, 10th Regiment, National Guard, New York. He is standing for his portrait with what appears to be the New York State Faithful Service Medal around his neck. His length-of-service chevrons on the cuff of his coat indicate years of service in the guard. The image dates from the 1910–1917 period. (Anthony Gero collection).

The caption of this postcard states that it is of "Co. M. 10th Rgt. Drilling at Camp Whitman N.Y." The card is dated 1916. According to the 1908 *SNY Adjutant General's Report*, Company M, 10th Regiment, was the former 14th Separate Company. (Roger Sturcke collection.)

In this portrait, a sergeant of the 22nd Engineers, the former 22nd Regiment Infantry, National Guard, New York, is presented, around 1902–1906. The last gasp of dress uniforms occurred prior to World War I, and this uniform of dark blue coat, with red and white piping, cuffs, and breast cords, designates his engineer's status. The photograph was by De Youngs, of Broadway and 17th Street, New York City. (Anthony Gero collection.)

This captain wears the last full-dress uniform before 1917. Note the embroidered New York State shield on his cap and his officer-style *NY* belt plate. Upon magnification, a 2 is seen on one of his medals, which may indicate membership in the 2nd Regiment, National Guard, New York. His rank is visible by the two gold bars on his shoulder knots. The image dates to 1902–1917. (Anthony Gero collection.)

After 1900, the uniforms of the country's various National Guards became the same as those worn by the U.S. Regular Army, the only difference being the use of state insignia. In this postcard, a private of Company L, 65th Regiment (Buffalo), shows this trend by his dress uniform around 1910–1917. The original image has his breast cords tinted light blue. (Anthony Gero collection.)

This unidentified mess detail shows several New York guardsmen around 1895–1902 with the tools of their cooking duties. Their unit is unidentified, but the patches on both sleeves of their dark blue shirts link them to New York. The letters appear light in color and are likely white. (Roger Sturcke collection.)

This postcard dates from around 1902–1914. Notice the distinctive drab shirts with "N.Y." on each sleeve and the "10N.Y. G" stenciled on the tent behind the men on the left. The two men standing in the middle hold what appears to be money, and in front of them, one man holds a baseball and another has a catcher's mitt. Possibly, the group received the money for winning a baseball game. (Anthony Gero collection.)

The caption on this card indicates that Company M of an unidentified unit is shown around 1910. One man appears to have on a baseball team uniform. The African American inside the cook tent on the right is not a member of New York's military. The postcard bears an Auburn postmark and lists a Cato photographer on the reverse. (Anthony Gero collection.)

Upon examination of this postcard image, several metal numbers 3 and letters M are visible on these soldiers' campaign hats around 1902–1908. Their hat cords appear a light color, probably white. They wear the older-style dark blue shirts with white *NY* sleeve patches. Their weapons appear to be Krag rifles, which were used in those years. Company M, 3rd Regiment, National Guard, New York, was from Cayuga County. (Anthony Gero collection.)

On the back of this postcard is written, "Non-commissioned officers Troop A Camp 1910," and on the front is written, "#2459, Troop A NCO, Gettysburg, July 1910." The soldiers are likely members of Troop A, New York, National Guard, from New York City, in field dress. Under magnification, the letter A is visible on their campaign hats and *NYNG* is stenciled on the tent. (Roger Sturcke collection.)

This photograph is labeled "1st Field Hospital." Under magnification, the stencil "First Field Hospital N.G.N.Y." can be seen on the lead wagon's canvas covering. The image likely dates from the years 1910 to 1916. It is a rare view of an early field hospital on the march. (Roger Sturcke collection.)

In an image titled "Co. M. 3rd Infantry N.G. N.Y. Auburn 1913," the company stands in formation at the train station in front of Auburn Prison, a New York State prison facility. The company's officers and men appear in field order. The civilian standing with them is unidentified. This photograph was taken by E. J. Kraemer of 176 East Genesee Street, Auburn. (Collection of the Cayuga Museum.)

Dated 1915, this postcard shows the entire 1st Brigade, National Guard, New York, in review at Camp Whitman, in formation for the governor's inspection. Notice the field musicians and band in the foreground. The mounted staff officers are in front of the brigade, which stands ready for its review. (Anthony Gero collection.)

Titled "Co. K. 23rd. N.Y. Inf. - Pharr, Tex. 8/8/16," this image shows guardsmen posing for a real-life photograph along the border with Mexico. The United States Army's 6th Division was made of New York guardsmen sent down to help police the border in 1916 by presidential order. (Anthony Gero collection.)

This postcard snapshot is identified by the markings on the wagon: "QuarterMaster 4th Brigade N.G. N.Y." Since railroad cars are seen in the background, the image may be of New York's National Guardsmen on service in Texas in 1916. (Anthony Gero collection.)

The caption of this large photograph states, "Troop M First New York Cavalry McAllen Texas 1916." Note the M on the stable building to the right. (Anthony Gero collection.)

These men represent Company G, 3rd Battalion, 3rd Regiment, from Rochester. During the 1916–1917 basketball season, the Centrals won their league's championship. Notice the full-dress uniforms of the seated officer and sergeant. One wonders how many of these men survived World War I, when this company became part of the 108th Infantry, 27th Division, American Expeditionary Force, which fought in France. (Anthony Gero collection.)

Four

NEW ADJUSTMENTS 1917–1960

According to the caption of this postcard, the 34th Company, 8th Regiment, Coast Defense Corps (the old 8th Regiment, National Guard, New York), is seen on the march to Fort Toten in August 1917. During the years from 1917 to 1919, the 8th Regiment helped to man the artillery defenses of New York's harbor and was not sent overseas. (Roger Sturcke collection.)

In 1917, Company M, 3rd Regiment, New York, National Guard, was ordered to Fort Niagara at Youngstown. This postcard shows Company M at Fort Niagara. Eventually the 3rd Regiment was sent to New York City, redesignated as the 108th Infantry, United States Army, and assigned to the 27th Division. Company M was from Cayuga County. (Roger Sturcke collection.)

In this postcard snapshot, a private of the 27th Infantry Division, American Expeditionary Force, poses for a photograph. The 27th Division was made up of all National Guard units from New York State; therefore, it is safe to say that this soldier was a member of a guard unit, although he is not identified. The *T* on his overseas cap's disk means he was in the division's ammunition train. (Anthony Gero collection.)

The 27th Division was an all–National Guard division from New York State assigned to the American Expeditionary Force. Gen. John F. O'Ryan and his staff are seen in this undated image, probably on shipboard, either going to France or returning home. (Roger Sturcke collection.)

In this image from about 1919, Capt. William Hodder poses. Before 1917, he had commanded Company M, 3rd Regiment. While in France, he was Company M's commander while the unit served in the 108th Infantry. A decorated war veteran, Hodder returned to the National Guard during the 1920s and became Auburn's assistant postmaster in 1931. (Collection of the Cayuga Museum.)

In 1915, New York finally rectified its exclusiveness and authorized the 15th Regiment, National Guard, New York, which consisted mainly of African American New Yorkers. Federalized in 1917 and redesignated the 369th United States Infantry, it fought bravely in France. This undated sheet music cover shows Lt. James Reese Europe, the 369th United States Infantry's bandleader during the war. Band members in the background wear military styles prevalent in the 1920s or 1930s. (Anthony Gero collection.)

African Americans served in the 369th United States Infantry, but this soldier who served in the 2nd Army in France is not a 369th member. The portrait, which bears a New York City photographer's mark, shows an African American New Yorker who served between 1917 and 1919. Observe the soldier's overseas stripes, one for each six months of overseas duty, on his coat's sleeve. (Anthony Gero collection.)

A series of postcards was created to document the homecoming of Cayuga County's veterans parade on April 1, 1919. This card shows part of that parade, held despite a spring snowfall. Many Cayugans had served in the 108th United States Infantry, the old Company M, 3rd Regiment. Members of the New York Guard, a home-defense unit, are seen here along the parade route. (Anthony Gero collection.)

This large print shows discharged soldiers at Canton (St. Lawrence County), outside of the Presbyterian church in that village. Some of these men had served in the National Guard, New York, prior to 1917. Note the 27th Division's patch on some of their uniforms. As one can see from the church's program board, a memorial service was being held in their honor. (Anthony Gero collection.)

This postcard bears the notation "Co. F, 174th Inf Peekskill, NY 1924," whose members were from the old 74th Regiment from Buffalo. During World War I, the 74th Regiment became the 174th United States Infantry. After the war, the 174th United States Infantry was reconstituted as an infantry regiment in the New York, National Guard. (Anthony Gero collection.)

This postcard's title reads, "Troop D. N. G. S. N. Y., Syracuse, N.Y." Following the end of World War I and during the early 1920s, the 121st Cavalry, National Guard, after various redesignations, was formed in the Upstate New York area. Troop D was based in Syracuse, Onondaga County. Note that the National Guard, New York, officially became the New York, National Guard, after World War I. (Anthony Gero collection.)

Pine Camp, now called Fort Drum, near Watertown, was, and still is, a training facility that is used by New York's National Guard. Around 1924, a battery of the newly formed 156th Field Artillery, New York, National Guard, poses in this photograph. As seen on the battery's guidon of red cloth with gold markings, which depict crossed cannons and regimental affiliations, these mounted artillerymen are from Battery C. The lineage of the 156th Field Artillery goes back to the 1st Regiment, New York Volunteers, formed in 1898. (Roger Sturcke collection.)

Various 1920s *New York Adjutant General's Reports*, along with Col. DeWitt Clinton Falls's National Guard studies, indicate a revival of regimental dress in some New York units after the war. In this early-1920s image from New York City, the front group wears an 1880s-style dress, while the next wears 1902–1910 uniforms. The age of some of these men suggests that they are part of a veterans' group. (Roger Sturcke collection.)

This photograph shows the red full-dress uniform adopted by the 22nd Engineers, New York, National Guard, in the 1920s. Note the 22 on their shako plates. These uniforms were not supplied by state authorities but were paid for out of regimental funds. These uniforms should not be confused with regimental dress from Victorian/Edwardian age, which can happen when one is unfamiliar with the 1920s revival of regimental dress uniforms. (Roger Sturcke collection.)

By the 1930s, uniforms had become more utilitarian. In this postcard view, Battery A, 212th Coast Artillery (from the old 12th Regiment, New York, National Guard) display its unit's association while at Fort Ontario, Oswego, used as a summer training facility by the guard. Some men wear the lapeled coats that were adopted by the U.S. Regular Army in 1926–1928 and became standard in New York's National Guard in the 1930s. (Anthony Gero collection.)

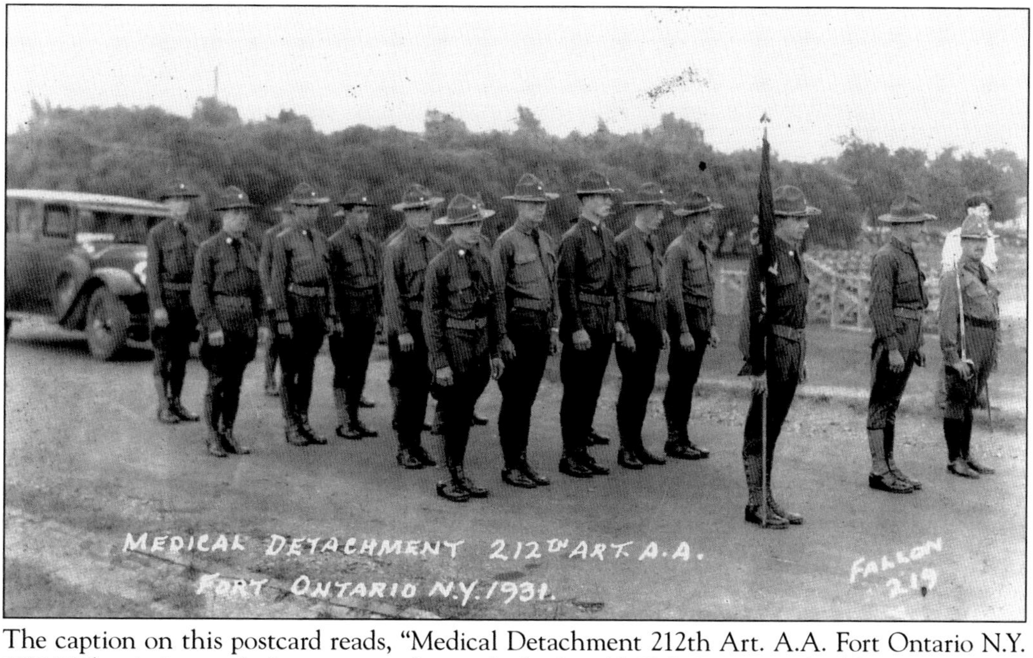

The caption on this postcard reads, "Medical Detachment 212th Art. A.A. Fort Ontario N.Y. 1931." The A.A. stands for antiaircraft, to which the old 12th Regiment had been converted. Note the detachment's guidon, which lies limp and does not reveal its medical insignia; also notice that the detachment's commanding officer carries a sword. (Roger Sturcke collection.)

This snapshot has on the reverse, "Taken Aug 15 1934 Camp Smith Company B" and shows the summer dress uniform of the 107th Regiment, New York, National Guard (of the old 7th Regiment). Notice the white hat cover, the white trousers, and the famous gray and black coat, long associated with the regiment. The 107th Regiment was one of the regiments that revived dress uniforms in the 1920s and 1930s. (Roger Sturcke collection.)

This postcard reads, "Co E 107th NYNG" and shows members of that unit around the 1930s. Notice that some men wear the gray trousers with black stripes and gray cap, which were worn as winter dress. All cross belts and body belts seen are made of white material. Officers wore a blue dress coat in this time period. (Roger Sturcke collection.)

In each regiment, Company M was designated as the machine gun company. This postcard's caption states, "Co M–107th 7–34." Notice the machine gun belts and ammunition boxes surrounding these soldiers from the 107th Regiment, posing in camp in July 1934. The regiment's crest in metal is also seen on some of their campaign hats. (Anthony Gero collection.)

Troopers of B Troop, 121st Cavalry, New York, National Guard, pose in their dress uniforms for this snapshot. The troop guidon of a red-over-white pennant is visible, with regimental numbers in gold. For mounted units, their dress hat had an additional chinstrap with buckle, for use on horseback. The image dates from the 1930s or early 1940. (Anthony Gero collection.)

This postcard shows F Troop, 121st Cavalry, at its guard mount at Pine Camp in the summer of 1932. Note the sabers of the troopers being presented during the posting. F Troop was from Buffalo. The 121st Cavalry was formed from across the upstate and western New York region in places like Geneseo, Syracuse, Rochester, Buffalo, and so on. (Roger Sturcke collection.)

This postcard reads, "Co C 108th" and shows members of the 108th Regiment, New York, National Guard, in the field in the 1930s. Note the regimental crest made of metal that is worn on the front of their campaign hats. The 108th's lineage goes back to the 3rd New York Volunteers of 1898, the 3rd Regiment of 1900–1917, and the 108th Regiment of 1917–1919. (Roger Sturcke collection.)

In this large panorama photograph, Company I, 108th Infantry of the New York, National Guard, proudly poses for a portrait during training at Fort McClellan, Alabama, in March 1941. Note the regimental crests visible on the garrison caps. Company I was from Auburn and Cayuga County and traces its lineage back to the 2nd Separate Company of 1881. Ultimately these Company I soldiers were sent to the Pacific as part of the 27th Infantry Division, United States Army. In September 1942, the 108th Infantry was assigned to the 40th Infantry Division in the Pacific Theater. (Anthony Gero collection.)

When the New York, National Guard, was federalized during World War II, it was replaced by the New York Guard, re-formed in 1940. As a volunteer home-defense force, it should not be confused with the New York, National Guard. One upstate regiment raised was the 3rd Regiment, New York Guard, with Company I from Cayuga County. The New York Guard's distinctive blue-black *NY* patch is visible on their uniforms. (Anthony Gero collection.)

This postcard shows additional members of the 3rd Regiment, New York Guard. Note the ages of these men, many of whom seem to be in their 30s and 40s; also note the sunglasses on several members. One man has a slung weapon that could be a Thompson machine gun, which was carried by selected members of the New York Guard. Each has an *NYG* patch on his garrison cap. (Anthony Gero collection.)

This postcard's title reads, "#117 Hq. Det. and Co C 3rd Regt. N.Y.G." Most of the men are in one-piece overalls or coveralls. Note the *NY* patches on their uniforms and garrison caps. The picture was probably taken at Peekskill, during the summer, while the 3rd Regiment, New York Guard, was in training, sometime between 1941 and 1946. (Anthony Gero collection.)

This postcard image is of members of Company I, 3rd Regiment, New York Guard, as the caption states. It was probably taken at Peekskill during training sometime between 1941 and 1946. (Anthony Gero collection.)

This group of officers is from the 74th Regiment, New York Guard, out of the Buffalo area. The photograph was taken sometime between 1940 and 1946. Note the Sam Browne belts worn by some of the officers. This style of belt was worn by U.S. Regular Army officers, National Guard officers, and New York Guard officers as a status of their rank between 1917 and 1946. (Anthony Gero collection.)

This group of officers is from the 74th Regiment, New York Guard, probably photographed during the summer between 1941 and 1948. Notice the summer pith helmet worn by two of the officers. A sign reading "Capt. Culligan" sits upon the table in front of their tent. It is safe to assume that one of these officers may be that man. (Anthony Gero collection.)

Following World War II, the 107th Infantry, New York, National Guard, the previous 7th Regiment, New York State Militia, whose lineage goes back to 1806, revived its striking dress uniforms of the 19th century. In this portrait, a private of Company L shows the gray and black regimental dress reintroduced in the 1950s. His black shako has white cording, white plume, and the regiment's pattern crest on the front. In 2006, the 200th anniversary of the 7th Regiment was celebrated. On special occasions, this 1950s dress is still seen when the 107th Infantry parades. (Anthony Gero collection.)

Selected Bibliography

Annual Report of the Adjutant-General of the State of New York for the Year 1879, transmitted to the Legislature January 14, 1880. Albany, NY: 1880.

The Company of Military Historians. *The Military Collector and Historian.* Rutland, MA: The Company of Military Historians, 1949–2006.

The Company of Military Historians. *Military Uniforms in America.* Rutland, MA: The Company of Military Historians, 1949–2006.

Gero, Anthony, and Roger Sturcke. *Cayugans in the Field, 1793–2003: Citizen Soldiers of Cayuga County, New York.* Auburn, NY: The Jacobs Press, 2004.

History of the 71st Regiment, N.G., N.Y. (American Guard). New York: Veterans Association, 71st Regiment, National Guard, New York, 1919.

Illustrated History 30th Separate Company, National Guard. New York: 1896.

Judson, Henry P. *A History of the Troy Citizens Corps.* Troy, NY: 1884.

Laws and Regulations for the Government of the National Guard of the State of New York. Albany, NY: Weed, Parsons and Company, 1885.

Martin, Major Clarence S., O.D.S.S.N.Y.N.G. *Three Quarters of a Century with the Tenth Infantry, New York National Guard, 1860–1935.* Albany, NY: J. B. Lyon, State Printer, 1935.

New York in the Spanish-American War, 1898, Part of the Report of the Adjutant-General of the State for 1900, in three volumes. Albany, NY: J. B. Lyon, State Printer, 1900.

Sawicki, James A. *U.S. Army Lineage.* 7 volumes. Dumfries, VA: Wyvern Publications, 1977–1991.

The 74th Regiment, N.G., S.N.Y., 1899. Buffalo, NY: Valentin and Munchausen, 1899.

Squadron A: A History of Its First Fifty Years 1889–1939. New York: Association of Ex–Members of Squadron A, 1939.

State of New York. *Published Annual Reports of the Adjutant–General for the Years 1860 to 1930.* Albany, NY: State of New York.

Todd, Colonel Frederick P., U.S.G.R. (K Co.), and Major Kenneth C. Miller, N.Y.G.R. (M Co.). *Pro Patrica et Gloria: The illustrated story of the one hundred and fifty years of the Seventh Regiment of New York (107th Infantry Regiment, NY, NG).* Hartsdale, N.Y.: Rampant House, 1956.

Todd, Frederick P. with Maria P. Todd/Damerel, Michael J. McAfee, Lee A. Wallace, Jr., and George Woodbridge. *American Military Equipage 1851–1870.* Vol. 2, *State Forces.* Chatham Square Press, Inc., 1983.

INDEX